Water, Water Everywhere

Water, Water Everywhere

Mark J. Rauzon and Cynthia Overbeck Bix

Sierra Club Books for Children • San Francisco

The Sierra Club, founded in 1892 by John Muir, has devoted itself to the study and protection of the earth's scenic and ecological resources—mountains, wetlands, woodlands, wild shores and rivers, deserts and plains. The publishing program of the Sierra Club offers books to the public as a nonprofit educational service in the hope that they may enlarge the public's understanding of the Club's basic concerns. The Sierra Club has some sixty chapters in the United States and in Canada. For information about how you may participate in its programs to preserve wilderness and the quality of life, please address inquiries to Sierra Club, 730 Polk Street, San Francisco, CA 94109.

First Edition

Library of Congress Cataloging-in-Publication Data

Rauzon, Mark J.
   Water, water everywhere / by Mark Rauzon and Cynthia Overbeck Bix. —1st ed.
      p.   cm.
   Summary: Describes the forms water takes, how it has shaped Earth, and its importance to life.
   ISBN 0-87156-598-6
   1. Water—Juvenile literature. [1. Water.] I. Bix, Cynthia Overbeck. II. Title.
GB662.3.R38 1993
551.48—dc20   92-34521

Book and jacket design: Bonnie Smetts
Printed in Singapore
10 9 8 7 6 5 4 3 2 1

for Suzanne
and all the little raindrops everywhere

— *M.J.R.*

Earth, the water planet,

shines brightly in the blackness of space.

White clouds swirl all around it,

over oceans of deepest blue.

Water brings color and life to the earth.

Without it, our planet would be

dusty, dry, and dead.

Water is everywhere.
It washes the sky with rain
and rushes along in rivers.
It splashes down waterfalls
and sparkles in the dewdrops
caught on a spiderweb.

Water is part of every living thing.
The stems and leaves of plants,
the bodies of humans
and other animals —
all are made mostly of water.

Water changes its form
almost like magic.
When water is a liquid,
we can spray it from a garden hose
or watch it trickle down the windowpane
during a summer shower.

When water is boiling hot,
it produces droplets called steam,
which we can see whistling
from the spout of a teakettle
or erupting from a hot spring
deep underground.

When it gets very cold,
water freezes into solid ice.
It may be as big as an iceberg
floating in the Arctic sea
or as small as the ice cubes
tinkling in a glass of lemonade.

The water on earth now
is the same water that was here
when earth began.

Water changes its form over and over
in a never-ending cycle.
It rises into the air
from oceans and lakes
as vapor, a gas we cannot see.
As it rises, the vapor cools
and turns back into tiny water droplets,
which form clouds.

As the clouds drift across the sky,
the droplets stick together
and fall back to earth as rain.
If the air is very cold, the rain freezes
and falls as hail, sleet, or snow.

Some of the rain and melting snow

soaks into the soil

and goes deep into the earth.

Some of it flows back

into rivers, lakes, and oceans.

Sooner or later, the same water

will turn into vapor again —

and it will begin its journey once more.

The movement of water

from the earth's surface

to the air

and back again

is a cycle that will go on forever.

Water is always moving
over the land, too.
A mountain spring
bubbles up out of the earth
and rushes down a mountainside.
On its way to lower ground,
the water splashes around rocks
and tumbles over waterfalls.

Farther down the mountain,
the little stream joins with others
to form a small river.
As more streams and rivers empty into it,
the current grows deeper and wider.
The river flows on over the land
until at last it meets the sea.

As water moves, it shapes the earth.

The muddy water of rivers

works like sandpaper.

Over millions of years,

it wears away solid rock,

cutting canyons deep into the earth.

High in the mountains

and in the coldest parts of the world,

snow builds up to form

deep fields of ice called glaciers.

As they slide slowly downhill,

glaciers pick up rocks and boulders

and, over thousands of years,

gouge out great valleys.

As ocean waves batter the shore,

little by little

they break down

the rocky cliffs

and grind them into sand.

Wherever water travels,

it brings the gift of life,

for all living things depend on water.

Trees and other plants grow thick

along waterways and beside lakes.

Rain helps keep forests and gardens

lush and green.

Thirsty animals drink their fill

and splash in cool water holes.

Some creatures,

like lobsters, fish, and whales,

spend their whole lives in water.

People depend on water, too.
We need clean, fresh water to drink,
and the basic foods for everyone on earth
need plenty of fresh water to grow.

People use water in many other ways.
We use it for cooking, washing, and bathing.
We use it to help make electricity
and to put out fires.
Water is also a handy "highway."
On boats of all kinds,
from dugout canoes to huge tankers,
people travel and carry goods
from place to place.
Because people depend on water,
we build our towns and cities
near lakes, rivers, and bays.

Water covers almost
three-fourths of the earth,
but nearly all of it is salt water.
Only a very small amount is fresh water —
and most of *that* is frozen in glaciers
near the North and South Poles.

The tiny bit of fresh water
that is not frozen
supports much of the plant
and animal life on earth.

Because we have such a small
supply of fresh water,
and because the number of people
who use it keeps growing,
we must learn to use our water wisely.

People waste water every day,
often without realizing it —
when we don't fix leaky faucets,
when we leave the water running,
when we take baths
instead of quick showers.

In many places, people are using water
faster than it can recycle itself.

We must also learn
to keep earth's water clean.
Cities dump tons of
waste into the ocean.
Factories empty harmful chemicals
into rivers, lakes, and bays.
Smoke from cars and industry
mixes with water vapor in the air
and falls to earth as acid rain.

All these things
pollute our water supply,
making it too dirty for people
and other animals to drink,
and too dirty for fish
and other creatures to live in.

Polluting our planet's water
spoils not just its usefulness,
but the beauty it brings to the earth.

We love to watch a clear lake
sparkling in the sun.
We tingle with the feel of cool water
flowing over our skin as we dive in.
We delight in catching
snowflakes on our tongues
and in skimming down
snowy mountain slopes on our skis.
We pause to hear the music
of a bubbling forest stream
or to breathe in the fresh,
salty smell of the sea.

Being near water

keeps us in touch

with the life of the earth.

CANADA

Lake of the
Woods

Northwest Angle

Rainy River

BWCAW
(Boundary Waters Canoe Area Wilderness)

Grand
Marais

Ely

Beaver
Bay

Lake Superior

Upper Red Lake

Lower Red Lake

NORTH DAKOTA

Red River of the North

Bemidji

Grand Rapids

Mississippi River

Duluth

WISCONSIN

Bois de Sioux River

Akeley

Lake Itasca
(headwaters of the
Mississippi River)

Mille
Lacs

Brainerd

Saint Croix River

N
E
W
S

Alexandria

Monticello

Minneapolis

Saint Paul

Minnesota River

Mississippi River

Winona

Minnesota River

SOUTH DAKOTA

Walnut
Grove

New
Ulm

Spring Grove

Pipestone
Nat'l.
Monument

IOWA

The Twelve Days of Christmas in Minnesota

written by
Constance Van Hoven

illustrated by
Mike Wohnoutka

STERLING

New York / London

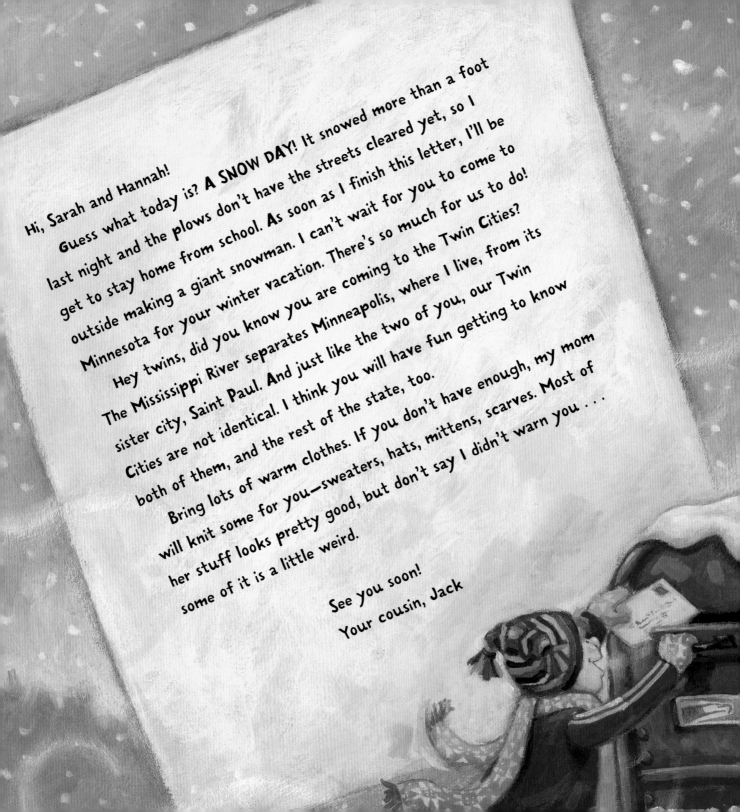

Hi, Sarah and Hannah!

Guess what today is? **A SNOW DAY!** It snowed more than a foot last night and the plows don't have the streets cleared yet, so I get to stay home from school. As soon as I finish this letter, I'll be outside making a giant snowman. I can't wait for you to come to Minnesota for your winter vacation. There's so much for us to do!

Hey twins, did you know you are coming to the Twin Cities? The Mississippi River separates Minneapolis, where I live, from its sister city, Saint Paul. And just like the two of you, our Twin Cities are not identical. I think you will have fun getting to know both of them, and the rest of the state, too.

Bring lots of warm clothes. If you don't have enough, my mom will knit some for you—sweaters, hats, mittens, scarves. Most of her stuff looks pretty good, but don't say I didn't warn you . . . some of it is a little weird.

See you soon!
Your cousin, Jack

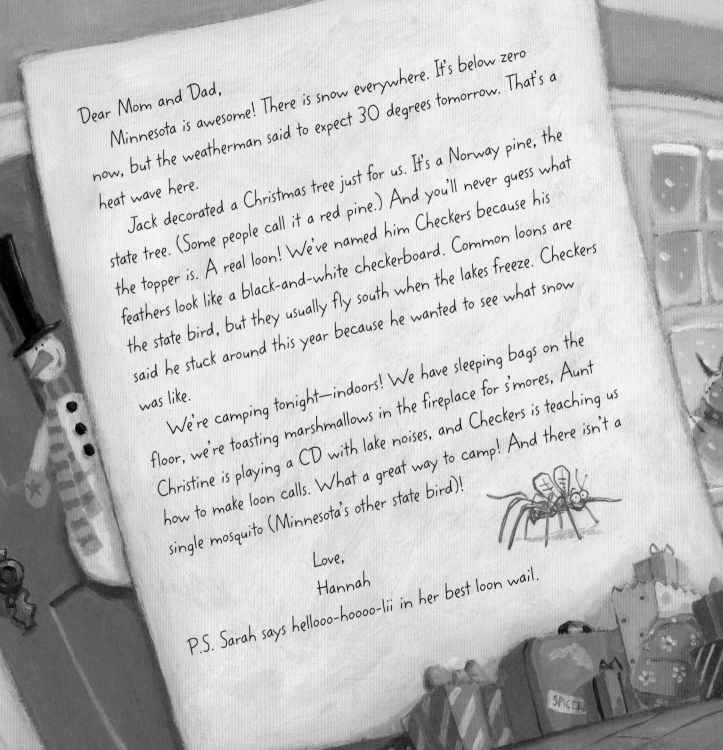

Dear Mom and Dad,

Minnesota is awesome! There is snow everywhere. It's below zero now, but the weatherman said to expect 30 degrees tomorrow. That's a heat wave here.

Jack decorated a Christmas tree just for us. It's a Norway pine, the state tree. (Some people call it a red pine.) And you'll never guess what the topper is. A real loon! We've named him Checkers because his feathers look like a black-and-white checkerboard. Common loons are the state bird, but they usually fly south when the lakes freeze. Checkers said he stuck around this year because he wanted to see what snow was like.

We're camping tonight—indoors! We have sleeping bags on the floor, we're toasting marshmallows in the fireplace for s'mores, Aunt Christine is playing a CD with lake noises, and Checkers is teaching us how to make loon calls. What a great way to camp! And there isn't a single mosquito (Minnesota's other state bird)!

Love,
Hannah

P.S. Sarah says hellooo-hoooo-lii in her best loon wail.

On the first day of Christmas,
our cousin gave to us . . .

a loon in a
Norway pine tree.

Dear Mom and Dad,

She shoots, she scores! Jack gave us hockey sticks so we could play ice hockey on a neighborhood rink. We had to wear protective pads, helmets, mouth guards, gloves, and, oh yeah, hockey skates. Good thing I had all that stuff on, because it didn't hurt (much) when I fell (lots)!!

Minnesota is called the State of Hockey. There are teams for all kinds of players. Kids my age play on Mite or Squirt teams. Funny names, huh?

Many Minnesotans have played on Olympic ice hockey teams. Jenny Potter has four Olympic medals, including a 1998 gold medal from the first women's ice hockey competition. In the 1980 Winter Olympics, more than half of the players on the men's gold-medal–winning United States team, plus the coach, were Minnesotans. Their win was called the Miracle on Ice. No one thought they could beat the Soviets, who were the best team in the world—but they did.

Sarah is outside practicing her slap shot. She says she wants to be a miracle on ice!

Love,
Hannah, the not-so-dyno-MITE

On the second day of Christmas,
our cousin gave to us . . .

2 hockey sticks

and a loon in a Norway pine tree.

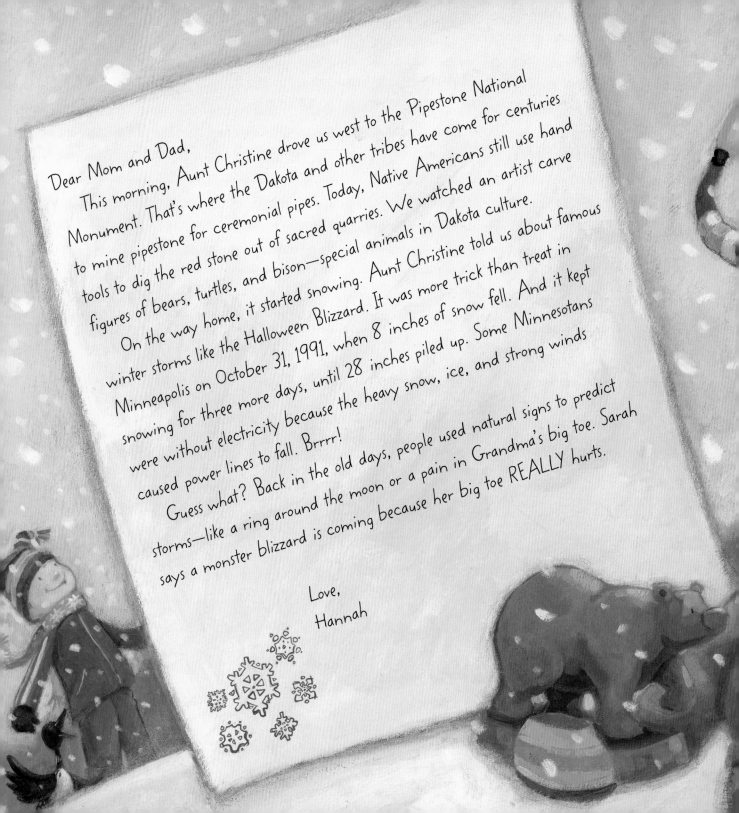

Dear Mom and Dad,

This morning, Aunt Christine drove us west to the Pipestone National Monument. That's where the Dakota and other tribes have come for centuries to mine pipestone for ceremonial pipes. Today, Native Americans still use hand tools to dig the red stone out of sacred quarries. We watched an artist carve figures of bears, turtles, and bison—special animals in Dakota culture.

On the way home, it started snowing. Aunt Christine told us about famous winter storms like the Halloween Blizzard. It was more trick than treat in Minneapolis on October 31, 1991, when 8 inches of snow fell. And it kept snowing for three more days, until 28 inches piled up. Some Minnesotans were without electricity because the heavy snow, ice, and strong winds caused power lines to fall. Brrrr!

Guess what? Back in the old days, people used natural signs to predict storms—like a ring around the moon or a pain in Grandma's big toe. Sarah says a monster blizzard is coming because her big toe REALLY hurts.

Love,
Hannah

On the third day of Christmas,
our cousin gave to us . . .

3 red stones

2 hockey sticks,
and a loon in a Norway pine tree.

Dear Mom and Dad,

No blizzard yet. Maybe Sarah's toe is sore from her new skates. Today we were hot on the trail of the legendary Paul Bunyan. Other states claim to be the birthplace of the giant lumberjack, but Minnesota is where Paul got serious about cutting trees. And everywhere Paul and his big blue ox, Babe, stepped, they made another lake!

We started in Brainerd by saying hello to a talking Paul, went on to Akeley to see the world's largest Paul (25 feet tall KNEELING!), and then over to Bemidji to see the oldest statue of Paul. Built in 1937, this Paul weighs 2.5 tons. Sometimes people decorate him and Babe with clothing. (You-know-who couldn't resist knitting Babe a scarf!)

Finally, we visited the Forest History Center in Grand Rapids and met a real live lumberjack. Guess what his name was? Paul! He told us that in 1900, all the lumber cut in Minnesota could have circled the earth! We saw the bunkhouse where Paul sleeps and the cook shack where he eats. The flapjacks smelled delicious.

Love,
Hannah

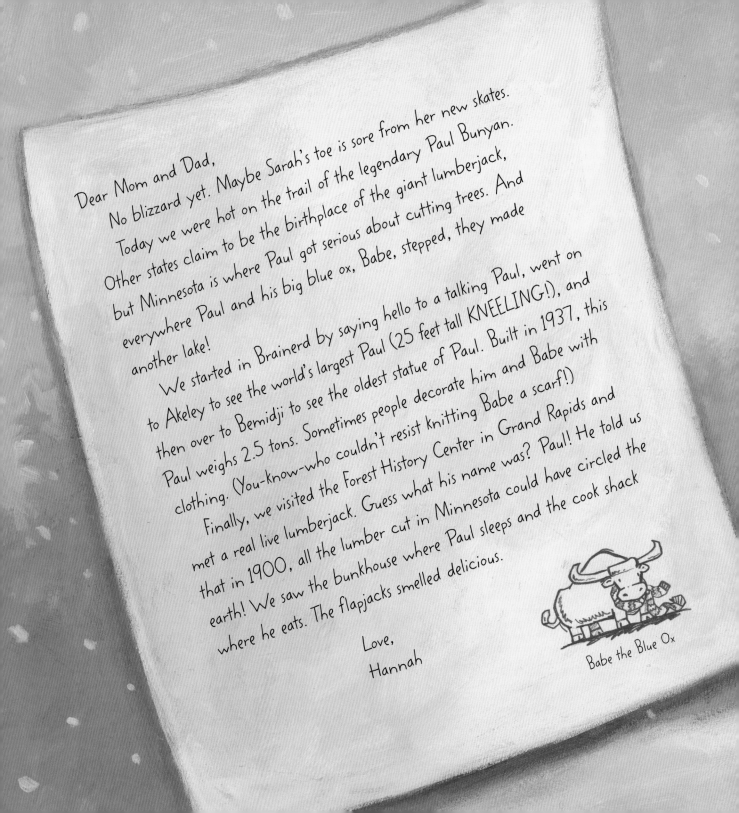

Babe the Blue Ox

On the fourth day of Christmas, our cousin gave to us . . .

4 lumberjacks

3 red stones, 2 hockey sticks,
and a loon in a Norway pine tree.

Dear Mom and Dad,

Did you know that Minneapolis was once the flour milling capital of the world? We toured an old flour mill in downtown Minneapolis, now the Mill City Museum. We loved the eight-story freight elevator ride. Every time the doors opened, we learned something new about milling.

When we got home, we baked Minnesota-shaped cutout cookies. Sarah nibbled off all the Northwest Angles. The Angle is the "chimney" at the top of the state. It is actually separated from the rest of Minnesota by the Lake of the Woods, so you can't get to the Angle area by car without going through Canada. Talk about map problems! It took more than 100 years for the United States and Great Britain to agree on this bit of zig-zag border.

For dinner, Jack made five hotdishes (aka casseroles). Wild Rice with Chicken is Jack's specialty, but I gave his Hamburger Hotdish a 10, too. Sarah voted for Super Duper Cheesy Macaroni, and Veggies Topped with Potato Nuggets. Checkers' favorite? Tuna Noodle Surprise.

Love,
Hannah, who is going to explode!

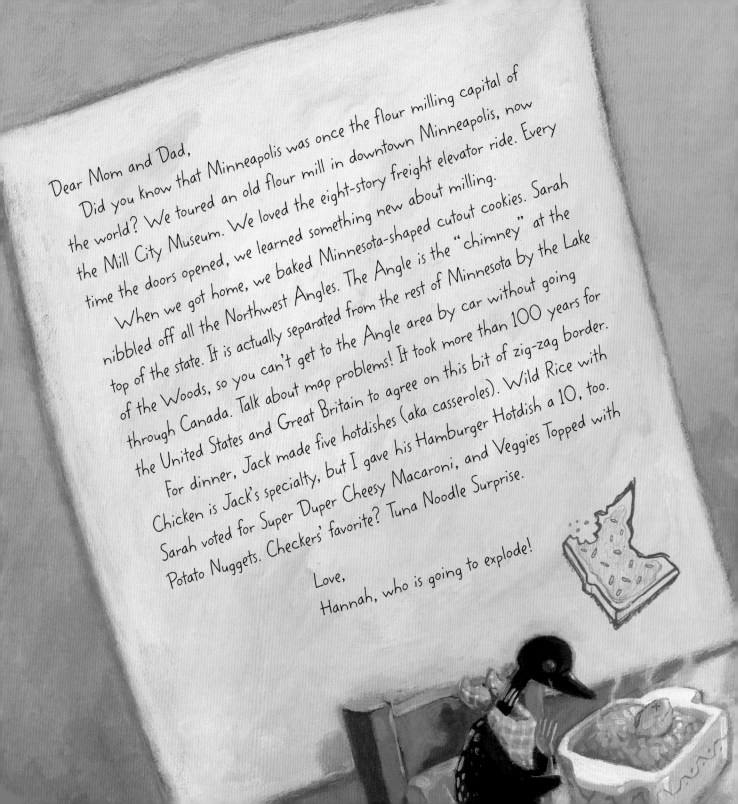

On the fifth day of Christmas, our cousin gave to us . . .

5 golden hotdishes

4 lumberjacks, 3 red stones,
2 hockey sticks,
and a loon in a Norway pine tree.

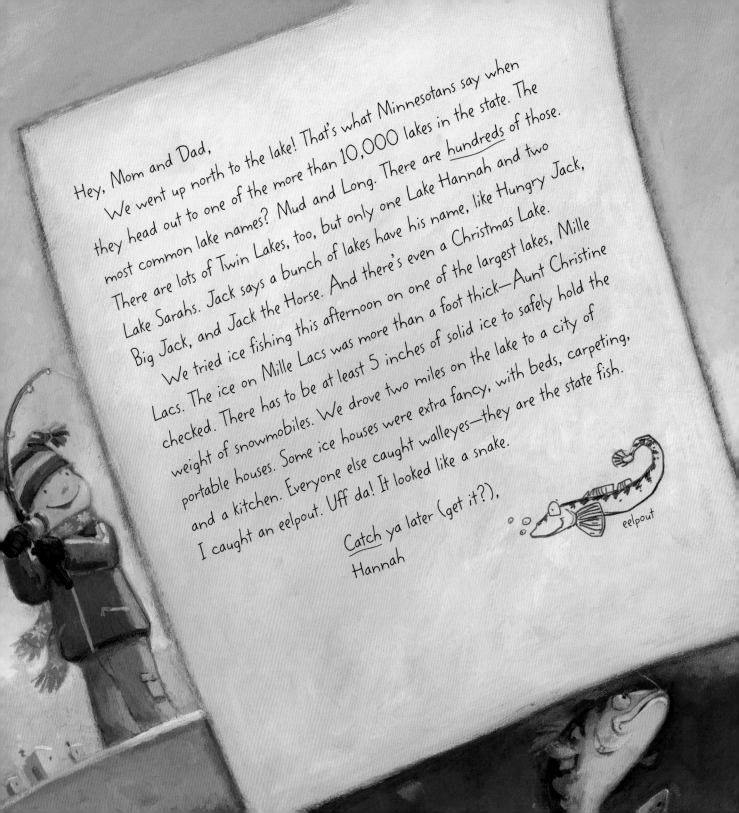

Hey, Mom and Dad,

We went up north to the lake! That's what Minnesotans say when they head out to one of the more than 10,000 lakes in the state. The most common lake names? Mud and Long. There are <u>hundreds</u> of those. There are lots of Twin Lakes, too, but only one Lake Hannah and two Lake Sarahs. Jack says a bunch of lakes have his name, like Hungry Jack, Big Jack, and Jack the Horse. And there's even a Christmas Lake.

We tried ice fishing this afternoon on one of the largest lakes, Mille Lacs. The ice on Mille Lacs was more than a foot thick—Aunt Christine checked. There has to be at least 5 inches of solid ice to safely hold the weight of snowmobiles. We drove two miles on the lake to a city of portable houses. Some ice houses were extra fancy, with beds, carpeting, and a kitchen. Everyone else caught walleyes—they are the state fish. I caught an eelpout. Uff da! It looked like a snake.

<u>Catch</u> ya later (get it?),
Hannah

eelpout

On the sixth day of Christmas,
our cousin gave to us . . .

6 walleyes wriggling

5 golden hotdishes, 4 lumberjacks,
3 red stones, 2 hockey sticks,
and a loon in a Norway pine tree.

Great Big Bird Alert!!!!

Today we went birding along the Mississippi River and did we ever get lucky! Near Monticello, where the river stays open most of the winter, we saw seven trumpeter swans. They are the largest water birds in North America and maybe the noisiest, too. Yes, they really sound like trumpets.

Next we watched bald eagles soaring over the river. They have wingspans of up to 8 feet! Minnesota is the place to come to see eagles—there are more here than just about anywhere else in the United States.

Then we saw a beautiful great gray owl with yellow eyes. Great grays are among the world's largest owls. Checkers seemed jealous— maybe he wishes he had big yellow eyes instead of red ones.

From your cygnet (young swan),
Hannah

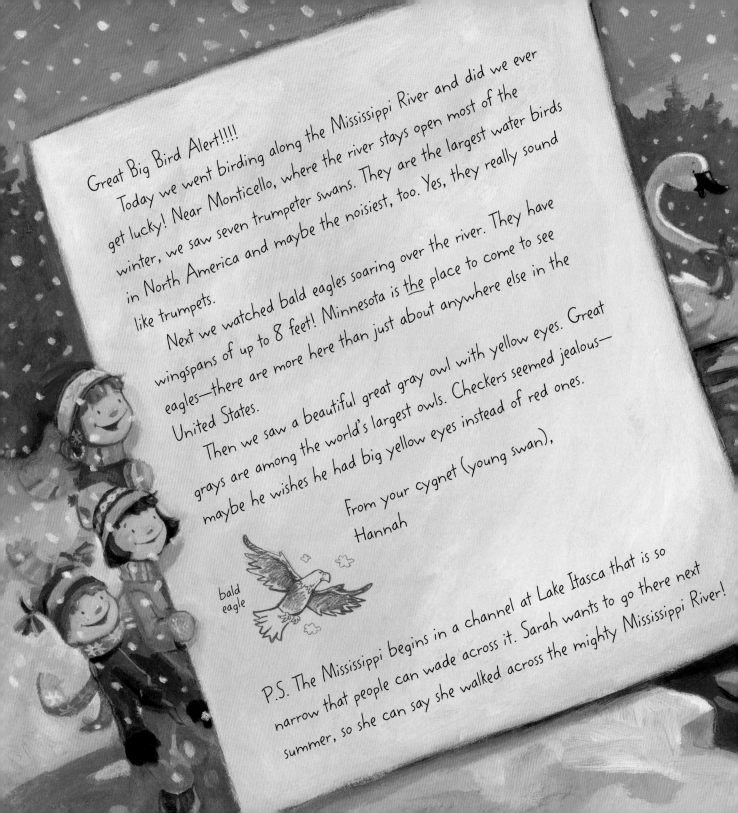

bald eagle

P.S. The Mississippi begins in a channel at Lake Itasca that is so narrow that people can wade across it. Sarah wants to go there next summer, so she can say she walked across the mighty Mississippi River!

On the seventh day of Christmas,
our cousin gave to us . . .

7 swans a-swimming

6 walleyes wriggling, 5 golden hotdishes, 4 lumberjacks,
3 red stones, 2 hockey sticks,
and a loon in a Norway pine tree.

Dear Mom and Dad,

Down on Grandpa's farm we met eight happy cows: Judy, Jane, Arlene, Tippi, Lea, Winona, Jessica B, and Jessica L. Grandpa says his Holsteins are named for Minnesota movie stars, because the cows are stars, too. Grandpa's stars produce more milk than any other cows in Spring Grove! And how does Grandpa keep his cows happy? He tells them lots of jokes, like this one about two Norwegian guys named Sven and Ole:

One hot summer day, Ole was painting his house. Sven stopped by and saw that Ole had on two winter coats. "Ole, why are you wearing those warm coats?" he asked. Ole's answer? "The instructions on the paint can said to put on two coats." HA! HA!

Grandpa told us his grandparents came from Norway. They taught him to like lutefisk (codfish soaked in lye). Sarah wouldn't try any because it smelled awful. I thought lutefisk tasted pretty good, especially with lots of butter from Grandpa's stars.

Love,
Hannah
(who is more Norwegian than Sarah!)

On the eighth day of Christmas, our cousin gave to us . . .

8 happy Holsteins

7 swans a-swimming, 6 walleyes wriggling, 5 golden hotdishes,
4 lumberjacks, 3 red stones, 2 hockey sticks,
and a loon in a Norway pine tree.

Dear Mom and Dad,

Minnesota has its share of amazing animals! Today we saw wolves WAY up north in Ely. Only Alaska has more wolves than Minnesota. Wolves are usually hard to see because they live deep in the forest. At the International Wolf Center, we watched four wolves through the windows and learned what wild wolves need to survive—space to roam and meat to eat.

At the North American Bear Center, the bears were hibernating, but we heard some bear facts: Minnesota has around 27,000 bears living in the wild, and cubs born in January and February weigh less than a pound!

At midnight, Aunt Christine called us outside to see the aurora borealis, or northern lights. Wow! Flickering green curtains rippled across the sky. Jack says that the lights are solar particles colliding with gases, and the farther north you go, the better chance you have to see them. All I know is the lights were GORGEOUS. Then a wolf started howling and Sarah's goose bumps grew as big as snowballs!

Love,
Hannah

On the ninth day of Christmas,
our cousin gave to us . . .

9 bears a-snoring

8 happy Holsteins, 7 swans a-swimming, 6 walleyes wriggling,
5 golden hotdishes, 4 lumberjacks, 3 red stones, 2 hockey sticks,
and a loon in a Norway pine tree.

Dear Mom and Dad,

Hike! Haw! Gee! We just went for an incredible dogsled ride in the Boundary Waters Canoe Area Wilderness, the BWCAW. It consists of more than a million acres of lakes and forests along Minnesota's border with Canada.

First, we learned all about Alaskan husky dogs—how much they love to pull, how much food they eat (lots!), and when they need to wear booties. The dogs were so excited they barked like crazy, but once we took off, all you could hear was the swish of sled runners, the dogs' breathing, and Sarah singing, "Over the river and through the woods to Grand Marais we go! The dogs know the way to carry the sleigh . . ."

Grand Marais is on the edge of Lake Superior, near a stop on the John Beargrease Sled Dog Marathon. This race honors a man who delivered mail by dogsled in the late 1800s. I'd like my mail to be delivered by my two favorite sled dogs: Yukon, with his beautiful blue eyes, and Nikki, who always seems to be smiling at me.

Love,
Hannah

On the tenth day of Christmas,
our cousin gave to us . . .

10 dogs a-dashing

9 bears a-snoring, 8 happy Holsteins,
7 swans a-swimming, 6 walleyes wriggling, 5 golden hotdishes,
4 lumberjacks, 3 red stones, 2 hockey sticks,
and a loon in a Norway pine tree.

Dear Mom and Dad,

Here we are at Lake Superior, the world's largest freshwater lake. Big ships loaded with iron ore, coal, and grain travel from Minnesota's port of Duluth to other ports on the Great Lakes or all the way out to the Atlantic Ocean. Lake Superior stays open much of the winter, thanks to boats called icebreakers. They clear shipping lanes of all but the thickest ice. CRRRUNCH!!

Terrible winter storms and gales have caused shipwrecks along the shore of Lake Superior north of Duluth. After several gales in 1905 killed people and sank ships, the Split Rock Lighthouse was built to steer ships clear of jagged rocks. The lighthouse sits on a 120-foot cliff and has a 54-foot tower, making it one of the tallest lighthouses on the Great Lakes. In 1910, two assistant lighthouse keepers drowned while sailing to Beaver Bay for mail. Jack says the ghosts of the young men still haunt Split Rock Lighthouse. Sarah says she won't be able to sleep tonight. Me neither!!

Love,
Hannah

Split Rock Lighthouse

On the eleventh day of Christmas,
our cousin gave to us . . .

11 spooky sailors

10 dogs a-dashing, 9 bears a-snoring, 8 happy Holsteins,
7 swans a-swimming, 6 walleyes wriggling, 5 golden hotdishes,
4 lumberjacks, 3 red stones, 2 hockey sticks,
and a loon in a Norway pine tree.

Greetings, Loyal Subjects:

We wish to stay longer in the kingdom of Minnesota. We still have places to go like the Children's Theatre in Minneapolis (it's the largest professional company of young actors in North America!) and things to do like snowshoeing and snow tubing (Jack says it's a blast). And our royal presence is totally required at the Saint Paul Winter Carnival!

Back in 1886, Saint Paulites wanted to celebrate what a great place their city was, even in winter. Local business owners created a carnival, and they've been holding it ever since, with a royal family, a treasure hunt, parades, and sculptors carving blocks of ice into beautiful statues. Sometimes they even construct a whole palace out of ice!

Jack plans to win the hotdish contest. Sarah wants to be a "bouncing girl" in the parade and get tossed high in the air on a blanket. All I need is a tiara . . .

Just call me Hannah, Queen of the Snows

P.S. Would it be okay if Checkers came home with us? He wants to meet his cousins, the Pacific loons.

snowshoe

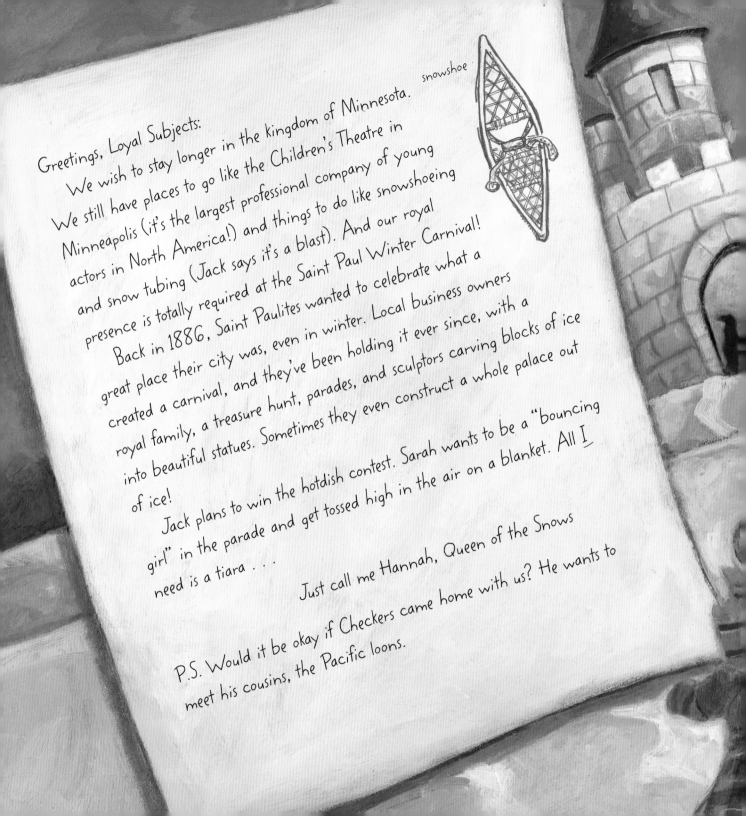

On the twelfth day of Christmas, our cousin gave to us . . .

12 sculptures sparkling

11 spooky sailors, 10 dogs a-dashing, 9 bears a-snoring,
8 happy Holsteins, 7 swans a-swimming, 6 walleyes wriggling,
5 golden hotdishes, 4 lumberjacks, 3 red stones,
2 hockey sticks, and a loon in a Norway pine tree.

Patty Berg
1918-2006
Golfer, Founding
member of LPGA

"Shop 'til you
drop at more
than 500 stores!"
Mall of America
Bloomington ★

Did Viking Explorers
visit Minnesota in 1362?
Kensington
Runestone
◆
Alexandria

F. SCOTT
FITZGERALD
1896-1940
FAMOUS
WRITER

Minneapolis
Sculpture
Garden

2 U.S. VPs

The
Children's
Theater

Walter
Mondale
from 1977-1981

Hubert
Humphrey
from 1965-1969

Agriculture

Crops: corn, sugar beets,
soybeans, wheat
Livestock: turkeys, hogs
dairy cows, cattle

Childhood home of
Laura Ingalls Wilder
~Walnut Grove~
Author of the
"Little House" books

WE
LL
ST
O

SOUL ASY

Q. Which town is not embarrassed
to be a cold spot in the nation?
A. Embarrass, MN (avg. of 64 days
per year of temps below 0°!)

Minnesota: Land of 10,000 Lakes

Capital: Saint Paul · **State abbreviation:** MN · **Largest city:** Minneapolis ·
State bird: the common loon · **State fish:** the walleye · **State flower:** the pink and white
showy lady's slipper · **State tree:** the Norway (red) pine · **State muffin:** blueberry ·
State drink: milk · **State motto:** "L'Etoile du Nord: The Star of the North"

Some Famous Minnesotans:

Ann Bancroft (1955–) was born in Mendota Heights. She is an Arctic adventurer and teacher, and the first known woman to cross the ice to the North and South Poles.

Bob Dylan (1941–) grew up in Duluth, where he taught himself to play guitar. Dylan is a singer, songwriter, and musician, famous for his protest songs of the 1960s. In 2008, he received a Pulitzer Prize Special Citation for his "profound impact on popular music."

Charles Lindbergh (1902–1974) was raised in Little Falls. In May 1927 he became the first person to make a solo, nonstop flight from New York to Paris in his plane, the *Spirit of St. Louis*. "Lucky Lindy" became an international hero after his famous flight of just under 34 hours.

Charles H. Mayo (1865–1939) and **William J. Mayo** (1861–1939), born in Le Sueur, were the sons of a frontier doctor. They became skilled physicians themselves, and founded the world-renowned Mayo Clinic in Rochester.

Mee Moua (1969–) was born in Laos and was nine years old when she came to the United States with her family. She is the first Hmong-American elected official in the United States. Her home is in Saint Paul, which has one of the largest Hmong communities of any U.S. city.

Dan Patch (1896–1916) lived in Savage for 14 years. Called the "King of Pacers," Dan Patch was a world-champion harness horse that never lost a race. His record for the fastest mile, set in 1906, has been equaled but never broken.

Charles Schulz (1922–2000) born in Saint Paul, drew the Peanuts comic strip for 50 years. His cartoon characters, Charlie Brown, Snoopy, Lucy, and the rest of the gang, are still loved by millions of fans around the world.

Roy Wilkins (1901–1981) spent his youth in Saint Paul and went to the University of Minnesota. He was an early civil rights leader who was the executive director of the National Association for the Advancement of Colored People (NAACP) for more than 20 years.